W9-ATF-085

FOR

MISSISSIPPI

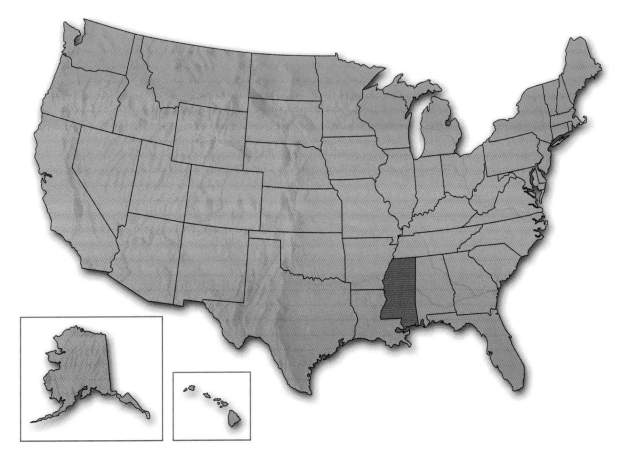

Jill Foran

Published by Weigl Publishers Inc.
123 South Broad Street, Box 227
Mankato, MN   56002
USA
Web site: http://www.weigl.com

Library of Congress Cataloging-in-Publication Data

Foran, Jill.
     Mississippi / Jill Foran.
       p. cm.
     Includes bibliographical references and index.
     ISBN 1-930954-70-0 (lib. bdg.)
      1. Mississippi--Juvenile literature. [1. Mississippi.] I. Title.

     F341.3 .F67 2000
     976.2--dc21   00-049936

Printed in the United States of America
1 2 3 4 5 6 7 8 9 10   05 04 03 02 01

Project Coordinators
Rennay Craats
Michael Lowry
Substantive Editor
Carlotta Lemieux
Copy Editors
Heather Kissock
Jennifer Nault
Designers
Warren Clark
Terry Paulhus
Layout
Mark Bizek
Photo Researcher
Jennifer Nault

Photograph Credits
Every reasonable effort has been made to trace ownership and to obtain permission to reprint copyright material. The publishers would be pleased to have any errors or omissions brought to their attention so that they may be corrected in subsequent printings.

Cover: Mansion (Mississippi Division of Tourism), Magnolia (Jerry Litton); **Archive Photos**: pages 6, 18, 21, 22, 25, 27; **Corbis Corporation**: pages 11, 14, 29; **Corel Corporation**: pages 3, 6, 7, 9, 13, 15, 20, 22, 23, 29; **Globe Photos**: pages 22, 24, 25; Hattiesburg Convention and Visitors Bureau: page 26; Historic Natchez Convention and Visitors Bureau: pages 8, 9, 16; **Jerry Litton**: pages 4, 10, 11, 14, 20, 26; **Memphis Public Library (Coovert Collection)**: page 19; **Mississippi Band of Choctaw Indians**: pages 20, 22; **Mississippi Department of Archives and History**: pages 17, 18, 19, 28; **Mississippi Division of Tourism**: pages 3, 6, 7, 8, 9, 12, 13, 15; **Mississippi Gulf Coast Convention and Visitors Bureau**: pages 4, 5, 25; **National Archives of Canada**: page 17 (C5400); **Photo Disc**: pages 26, 27; **University of Mississippi**: page 15; **Visuals Unlimited**: page 10.

CONTENTS

The blossoms of the magnolia tree come in a variety of colors from white to pink, yellow, and purple. Some blossoms can be as large as 14 inches in diameter.

INTRODUCTION

Mississippi is located in the Deep South of the United States. It is named after the Mississippi River, which forms most of its western border. An Algonquian group was among the first people to see the river. They gave it the name *Mississippi*, which means "great water" or "big water." The Mississippi River is the largest river in the United States. It runs through most of the country and empties out into the Gulf of Mexico. This great river is responsible for much of Mississippi's rich soil and **fertile** land.

Mississippi's nickname is the "Magnolia State." Beautiful magnolia trees grow throughout the region. Sweet-smelling flowers blossom on these trees. The magnolia is both the state tree and the state flower. Mississippi's stunning forests and rivers attract visitors from all over the world.

QUICK FACTS

Mississippi was the twentieth state to enter the Union. It was admitted into the United States on December 10, 1817.

Other nicknames for Mississippi include "Bayou State" and "Mud-cat State."

The capital of Mississippi is Jackson. It is in the central part of the state.

Mississippi's state waterfowl is the wood duck.

Canoeists have much to explore when paddling down the Mississippi River. The river is responsible for draining nearly thirty-one states.

Including all of its bays and inlets, the Mississippi Gulf Coast has a total length of 359 miles.

Getting There

Four other states in the Deep South border Mississippi. Tennessee lies to the north, Alabama to the east, Arkansas to the west, and Louisiana to the southwest. The Gulf of Mexico borders Mississippi's southeast region. This strip of land is best known as the Gulf Coast.

Many major highways connect to the Magnolia State. Mississippi's many waterways also make it possible to arrive by boat. The main ports along the Mississippi River are Vicksburg, Greenville, and Natchez. Two of the busier ports on the Gulf Coast are Pascagoula and Gulfport. There are more than 170 airports in the state with Jackson International Airport being the busiest. Passenger trains travel through about fifteen cities in Mississippi.

QUICK FACTS

Mississippi's state song is "Go Mississippi."

The state bird is the mockingbird. It is a popular bird in the south, as it also represents Arkansas, Florida, Texas, and Tennessee.

Mississippi covers over 48,000 square miles.

The state water mammal is the bottlenose dolphin.

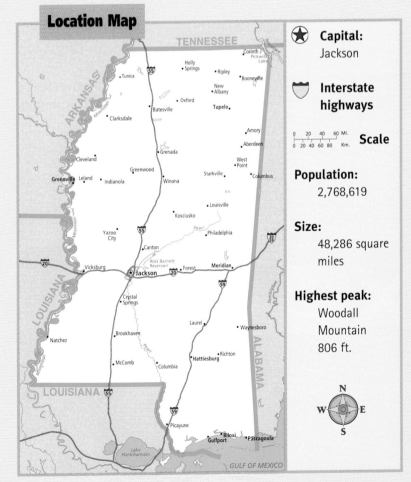

Location Map

TENNESSEE

ARKANSAS

LOUISIANA

ALABAMA

LOUISIANA

GULF OF MEXICO

Corinth
Pickwick Lake
Holly Springs
Ripley
Booneville
Tunica
New Albany
Oxford
Tupelo
Batesville
Clarksdale
Amory
Aberdeen
Grenada
West Point
Cleveland
Greenwood
Starkville
Columbus
Greenville Leland
Indianola
Winona
Louisville
Kosciusko
Yazoo City
Pearl
Philadelphia
Canton
Ross Barnett Reservoir
Vicksburg
Jackson
Forest
Meridian
Crystal Springs
Laurel
Waynesboro
Natchez
Brookhaven
Richton
Hattiesburg
McComb
Columbia
Picayune
Biloxi
Gulfport Pascagoula
Lake Pontchartrain

⭐ **Capital:**
Jackson

🛡 **Interstate highways**

0 20 40 60 Mi.
0 20 40 60 80 Km.
Scale

Population:
2,768,619

Size:
48,286 square miles

Highest peak:
Woodall Mountain 806 ft.

N
W E
S

Some early **plantation** owners brought Victorian traditions and styles to Mississippi.

Mississippi is probably most famous for its cotton history. In the 1800s, many settlers in the state became rich from growing cotton. They built splendid homes, some of which are still around today. As a result of all the wealth cotton brought to the state, it became known as "King Cotton." Eventually, the Civil War would bring an end to much of Mississippi's wealth.

Slavery was very much a part of the Deep South at this time. African-American slaves performed the back-breaking work of planting and picking the cotton. When states in the north threatened to end slavery many southern states—including Mississippi—were determined to keep it. This disagreement evolved into the Civil War. Even after the Civil War, when slavery was **abolished**, African Americans continued to suffer as a result of racial **segregation**. Not until the **civil rights movement** of the 1950s and 1960s did conditions begin to improve. During this time, Mississippi would play an important part in the fight for African-American rights.

The civil rights movement employed nonviolent marches to bring equal rights to African Americans.

QUICK FACTS

The Mississippi state flag still bears the Confederate markings of its past. The "Southern Cross," displayed in the upper left hand corner, was the official Confederate Battle Flag during the Civil War.

Mississippi's motto is "By Valor and Arms."

Historic homes like Rosalie, a mansion in
Natchez, are reminders of life in the Old South.

The state land mammal
is the white-tailed deer.

In 1962, James Meredith
became the first African
American to enroll in the
University of Mississippi.
Meredith had to be
protected from protesters
by federal marshals.

In the twentieth century, farm machines were
invented that could do many of the jobs once
done by laborers. As a result, countless
Mississippians were soon out of work. Despite
its great beauty, fertile soil, and southern
pride, Mississippi became one of the poorest
states in the nation.

Today, Mississippi is in a position of great
change. New industries are bringing money
into the state, and cotton now grows
alongside a wide range of other crops.
Mississippians still cherish the large
mansions and southern traditions of their
past, but they are now looking for new
ways to improve their lives and their
beautiful homeland.

**Cotton is produced on only about 10 percent of Mississippi's
farms. The other 70 percent of farms produce dairy and
livestock products.**

LAND AND CLIMATE

The Mississippi **Alluvial** Plain covers the western edge of the state. It is made up of broad, flat lowlands that were once the old **floodplains** of the Mississippi River. The Gulf Coastal Plain makes up the rest of the state. It has hills, stretches of marshy land, prairies, pinewoods, and plains. Offshore, there are several islands, which are popular with explorers, nature lovers, and sunbathers.

Mississippi's climate is warm and moist. The summers are hot and humid, with temperatures in July averaging 82 °Fahrenheit. Winds from the Gulf Coast and frequent thunderstorms help to cool the weather. Hurricanes sometimes sweep up from the Gulf Coast in the late summer months. Winters in Mississippi are mild, with abundant rainfall. Because of the warm climate, the Mississippi growing season is long and fruitful.

Rivers, swamps, and marshes cover the Mississippi landscape.

QUICK FACTS

At 806 feet, the top of Woodall Mountain is the state's highest point. It is actually just a large hill, since Mississippi has no mountains.

The highest temperature ever recorded in Mississippi was in Holly Springs on July 29, 1920. It was 115 °F.

The lowest temperature ever recorded in Mississippi was at Corinth on January 30, 1966. It was –19 °F.

During the 1927 Mississippi Flood, the town of Greenville was under water for seventy days.

The Alluvial Plain area is also known as the Delta.

The Coastal Plain extends from the Delta to the eastern edge of the state.

Water is one of Mississippi's most precious resources.

NATURAL RESOURCES

Soil and water are Mississippi's most plentiful natural resources. The state's many rivers and lakes provide it with large supplies of surface water as well as a number of wells. The lakes of Mississippi are not all natural. The larger lakes are a result of the many dams that were built to prevent river floods, which would damage crops and homes.

The floodwaters of the past were also responsible for positive changes. The soil in the Mississippi Delta is made up of **silt** deposited on the land by floodwaters. This alluvial soil is very good for growing crops, which is why cotton does so well there. Another very fertile area is the Black Belt, where the soil is mainly black in color. The Black Belt is a narrow stretch of land found in the northeastern part of Mississippi.

The fertile soils of Mississippi are partly a result of regular river floods in the past.

PLANTS AND ANIMALS

More than half of Mississippi's land is covered by forests. In the northern part of the state, the forests consist of tulip trees, sycamores, honey locusts, and many species of oak and hickory. Swamp oaks, bald cypresses, and tupelo can be found in the forests of the Delta. Many kinds of pine grow in the Piney Woods, which cover much of southern Mississippi. Pecan and magnolia trees grow throughout the state.

Foxes, raccoons, opossums, rabbits, squirrels, armadillos, and wild turkeys can all be found in the forests. Alligators lurk in many of the state's swampy areas. They share these damp places with turtles and frogs.

By opening large quantities of land to farming and hunting, much of the big game that once roamed the forests is now very scarce. The wolf, cougar, and bison have all disappeared from the Mississippi region.

An adult ringed sawback turtle has a yellow undershell and yellow markings on its head.

QUICK FACTS

There are many types of fish in Mississippi. Catfish, bream, bass, and perch are found in the state's fresh waters. Shrimp, oysters, and salt water fish swim in the Gulf of Mexico.

There is a haunted river in Mississippi. Strange sounds come from the Pascagoula Singing River. The sounds are believed to be the death chant of a Pascagoula group that committed mass suicide in the river to avoid surrendering to their enemies, the Biloxi.

Mississippi's swamps provide great homes to the many American bull frogs in the state. The American bull frog can jump up to nine times its body length.

QUICK FACTS

The Mississippi Petrified Forest is made up of giant trees and logs that date back 36 million years. Water once covered these woodlands, and the minerals in the water turned the wood to stone.

The Friendship Oak, in Long Beach, Mississippi, is a huge oak tree that is more than 500 years old and is more than 50 feet high. Its trunk has a **circumference** of 17 feet, and its branches and leaves give more than 16,000 feet of shelter.

Around 120 kinds of trees grow in Mississippi.

There was a time when nearly all of Mississippi was covered in forests. When settlers arrived, they cut down the trees to create farmland. As time passed, swamps were drained, and **levees** were built to control flooding. Many more trees were cut down for the lumber industry.

Today, the state has a program of planting young trees to replace those cut down for the lumber industry. Much of Mississippi's abandoned farmland has been replanted with trees. Other efforts to preserve Mississippi's forests and wildlife include setting up state and national parks and funding wildlife and nature preserves.

Soil **erosion** is a problem in Mississippi. The wind and weather have worn away the **topsoil** in some areas. In other areas, **gullies** have been eroded. Over the years, the farming of cotton has removed much of the land's fertility. To prevent further soil erosion and restore the fertility to the soil, large areas of eroded land have been planted with trees or turned into pasture.

Mississippi's lush pastures are due to its rich soil. The state's pastures are ideal for raising cattle.

TOURISM

The sunny beaches of the Gulf Coast are lined with large hotels, fine restaurants, and many tourist attractions. Visitors can see what life may have been like in Mississippi before the Civil War by visiting the mansions in Vicksburg or Natchez. During the tourist season, dozens of local mansions are opened to the public in Natchez.

In Vicksburg, tourists can also visit the National Military Park. This park preserves one of the most important battlefields of the Civil War—Vicksburg. The Vicksburg fortress guarded the Mississippi River, and when it fell Union forces gained full control of the river. Exhibits include re-creations of soldiers' quarters and the caves that civilians hid in during battles. Re-enactments of famous Civil War battles take place at certain war sites throughout the state.

Tourists can step even further back in time by visiting the Grand Village of the Natchez Indians. At the site visitors can explore the Grand Village museum. The museum offers educational programs to teach visitors about the history and the culture of the Natchez peoples.

The Vicksburg National Military Park has reconstructed trenches and rebuilt gunboats, which recreate the Vicksburg battlefield.

From late summer to early winter, mechanical pickers gather cotton bolls from fields in the Mississippi Delta.

INDUSTRY

For more than a century before World War II, Mississippi's economy was dominated by agriculture. Cotton was the main crop. After World War II, tractors, mechanical cotton pickers, and **combines** took the place of human laborers. Plantations which had provided jobs for dozens of families quickly became mechanized. Today, cotton plantations require only a few people to operate the machines. Cotton is still a leading crop, along with soybeans, but it is less important to the economy than it once was.

Manufacturing is now the main industry of the state. Mississippi makes a wide variety of goods, including clothing, foods, electronic equipment, lumber and wood products, and chemicals. Both the shrimp and catfish industries are also very profitable. The Mississippi Delta leads the nation in farm-raised catfish production, and the areas along the Gulf Coast are among the main suppliers of shrimp in the nation.

Some Mississippi farmers raise catfish in artificial ponds. Catfish ponds are made on land where crops have been growing poorly due to over-farming.

GOODS AND SERVICES

There are about 74,000 miles of highway in Mississippi. Highway 61, which passes through the Delta, is one of the most famous roads in North America. In blues songs, it is referred to as the route that musicians took to play shows in Chicago and New Orleans.

An even older roadway is the Natchez Trace Parkway. Maintained by the federal government, it twists and turns for more than 400 miles, from Natchez to Nashville, Tennessee. Hundreds of years ago, the Natchez Trace Parkway was a pathway used by First Nations hunters. Later, explorers and settlers would use it to travel between the Mississippi and Tennessee Rivers. Today, there are still places where you can walk parts of the original pathway. Granite markers identify the old trail, which is worn deep by countless people and horses.

In traditional blues music, the human voice is used to mimic the sound of certain instruments, particularly the harmonica and the guitar.

There is a paved road that now runs alongside the original Natchez Trace Parkway.

QUICK FACTS

Most of the early railways in Mississippi were destroyed during the Civil War. Mississippi's present rail network dates from the 1880s.

Twenty-four daily newspapers are published in Mississippi.

The John C. Stennis Space Center is in Mississippi. Here NASA tests engines for space shuttles and other rockets.

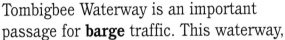

Highways and roads are not the only high traffic areas in Mississippi. The waters in Gulfport and Pascagoula are often crowded with oceangoing ships. Smaller boats travel up the Mississippi River to Natchez, Vicksburg, and Greenville. The Tennessee-Tombigbee Waterway is an important passage for **barge** traffic. This waterway, which opened in 1985, has become a chief shipping route in the east. It provides the state's growing industries with a quick and inexpensive route for shipping goods to ports along the Gulf Coast.

The hotels and resorts of the Gulf Coast provide many jobs in the service industry. Floating casinos are the newest addition. Gambling in Mississippi is only legal if it is done offshore, so boats have been built to house casinos. Since the first casino opened in 1992, at least a dozen more have been added. They draw people from all over North America and have given a big boost to Mississippi's economy.

Mississippi's floating casinos are popular among tourists who visit the state.

Today, many Natchez still live in Mississippi.

FIRST NATIONS

About 1,000 years ago, the Mississippi region was populated with Native Peoples known as Mound Builders. These peoples piled layers of dirt on top of big pits to form giant mounds. Some mounds served as burial sites, while others were places of worship. Chiefs and priests lived on special mounds, and their houses or temples stood above the villages. The Mound Builders are believed to have been a highly civilized society with great expertise in farming and architecture.

By 1500, the Mound Builders had disappeared, and three distinct First Nations groups dominated the region. The Choctaw lived mostly in central and southern Mississippi, the Chickasaw controlled the northern part of the region, and the Natchez dominated the southwest. In 1540, when the first European explorers arrived in the Mississippi region, about 30,000 Native Americans were living there.

Nobody is sure why the earliest Mound Builders disappeared.

Mounds were probably made over a period of several thousand years.

The word Choctaw means "charming voice."

Other Native peoples in the area included the Yazoo, Biloxi, and Pascagoula.

The Mississippi Band of Choctaw make many intricate arts and crafts.

The explorer Pierre Le Moyne joined the French navy when he was only fourteen.

QUICK FACTS

The first French settlement in Mississippi was at Ocean Springs, on the Gulf Coast.

British traders began arriving in the region around 1698. They were seen as a threat to the French settlers.

La Salle named the Mississippi Valley region Louisiana, after King Louis XIV of France.

EXPLORERS AND MISSIONARIES

Hernando de Soto, a Spanish explorer, was the first known European to visit the Mississippi area. In 1540, de Soto and his army passed through the northern region looking for gold. Some of his soldiers had smallpox and other diseases that were new to North America. Native Americans had no immunity to these diseases, and as a result, many died. De Soto and his men left the region without finding any gold.

The next Europeans to enter the Mississippi region arrived over one hundred years later. In 1682, a French explorer named René-Robert Cavelier, known as Sieur de La Salle, traveled down the Mississippi River to the Gulf of Mexico. He claimed the Mississippi region for France. In 1699, Pierre Le Moyne, also known as Sieur d'Iberville, established the first permanent settlement of Biloxi in Mississippi's southeast.

At first, the French got along with the Natchez people. But after a while, the settlers began to take over large portions of Natchez land. In 1729, the Natchez attacked Fort Rosalie in an effort to save their land. The French fought back. By 1731, almost every Natchez had been killed. This war became known as the Natchez Revolt.

When Hernando de Soto died, his aide sank the body in the Mississippi River to keep the news of his death from the Native Americans.

After the Treaty of Paris left France in terrible debt, the people turned against the king, Louis XVI, and sentenced him to the guillotine.

EARLY SETTLERS

Early attempts to colonize the Deep South proved disastrous. In the early 1700s, several thousand settlers were lured to the area by the promise of easy money. The colonial government was unable to provide for their needs, and many settlers starved to death.

The surviving settlers lived near the French forts, but their numbers remained small. Many people were unwilling to come to the region because of the frequent fighting in the area. There was almost constant war between the French and the British in Mississippi.

In 1763, the British won the French and Indian War. According to the Treaty of Paris, France was to hand Mississippi over to Britain. During the American Revolution, the Spanish took over the Gulf Coast, and it wasn't until the 1790s that all of Mississippi was in American hands.

QUICK FACTS

France sent Casquette girls to Mississippi in the early 1700s as wives for the settlers. Each girl received a small amount of money and a chest of clothes suitable for marriage.

The Treaty of Paris, signed in 1763 after the French and Indian War, gave the British all the land east of the Mississippi River. The Gulf Coast region became part of the British province called West Florida.

During the American Revolution, Spain claimed the Mississippi Gulf Coast from the British.

The Old Spanish Fort, built by Pierre Le Moyne's expedition, is thought to be the oldest structure between the Appalachian and Rocky Mountains.

Southern plantation owners were dependent upon African-American slaves for their profits.

In the late 1700s and early 1800s, thousands of settlers came to Mississippi from the more crowded states in the east. At first, they settled mostly in southern and west-central Mississippi. Northern Mississippi was controlled by the Choctaw and Chickasaw.

In the 1830s, the United States government made the Choctaw and Chickasaw sign treaties which gave up their land. After the treaties were signed, thousands of settlers from the eastern states came to farm the fertile soil.

The mid-1800s saw Mississippi settlers making huge profits from cotton on large farms called plantations. The plantation owners used slave labor in order to make their fortunes. Africans were brought to the United States by slave traders, and were forced to do the hard work of planting and harvesting the cotton.

By 1850, nearly two-thirds of the plantation slaves worked in the production of cotton.

POPULATION

Mississippi is mainly a rural state. Of the more than 2.7 million people that live in Mississippi, at least half of them live on farms or in small towns. In recent years, many Mississippians have moved to the cities in search of jobs.

Most people in Mississippi with a European background came from Britain, Ireland, or Northern Europe. Up until 1940, six out of every ten people in Mississippi were African American. After 1940, many African Americans moved to cities in the northern states in search of a better life. Now, only one in three people in Mississippi is African American. Despite these changes, Mississippi still has the highest percentage of African Americans in the United States.

The state of Mississippi is blessed with a rich African-American culture.

QUICK FACTS

A small Chinese population can be found in the Delta. The Chinese are descended from farm laborers who were brought to Mississippi from California in the 1870s.

The four largest cities in Mississippi are Jackson, Gulfport, Biloxi, and Hattiesburg. Jackson has by far the most people, with a population of 188,000.

A few thousand Choctaw still live in the east-central part of Mississippi.

POLITICS AND GOVERNMENT

Mississippi became a territory of the United States in 1798. In 1817, it became the twentieth state of the Union. The state's constitution of 1890 gave Mississippi three branches of government.

The legislative branch makes the laws. This branch consists of the Senate and the House of Representatives. There are 52 senators and 122 representatives. All are elected for four-year terms.

The second branch is the executive, headed by the governor. Like the other members of the executive branch, the governor is elected for a four-year term. The executive branch ensures that the laws are carried out.

The judicial branch sees that the laws are obeyed. It consists of the courts and their judges. The highest court in the state is the Supreme Court.

Some of Mississippi's old court houses are now museums.

QUICK FACTS

On June 12, 1963 Medgar Evers was assassinated in front of his home in Jackson. Evers was a **recruiter** for the National Association for the Advancement of Colored People. His death made him a symbol of the civil rights movement.

Today, Mississippi has a greater proportion of African-American elected officials than any other state in the nation.

The Mississippi State Capitol, built in 1903, is located in Jackson.

Mississippi still has a French population.

Jackson hosts the United States' second largest parade honoring Dr. Martin Luther King, Jr. Celebrations of Dr. Martin Luther King, Jr. Day occur statewide.

There is a more diverse blend of cultures in the coastal area of Mississippi than anywhere else in the state. On the coast, blends of French, Spanish, Latin American, and British heritages can be found.

CULTURAL GROUPS

There is a wide range of cultures in Mississippi. Many of these cultures can be seen in the southern part of the state, both in the buildings and in the local customs. French, Spanish, Latin-American, British, and African-American traditions are especially evident here.

African-American culture is very strong throughout Mississippi. Each year, Mississippi holds celebrations honoring African-American achievements, including the civil rights movement. African-American culture can be seen in everything from literature to food. It also had a strong influence on music. Blues music originated in the cotton fields of the Mississippi Delta. The music, which is based on African rhythms, originally focused on the sufferings of the plantation workers. The blues later became popular throughout the country.

Riley B. King, known to his fans as B.B. King, was born in 1925 on a cotton plantation in Itta Bene, Mississippi.

Mississippi's French Catholic heritage is very noticeable along the Gulf Coast.

Today, the blues remains one of the most important types of music in Mississippi. Famous Mississippi blues musicians include Bo Diddley, John Lee Hooker, Muddy Waters, and B.B. King. The Delta Blues Festival, held each fall in Greenville, honors famous blues musicians and showcases new ones.

The Choctaw celebrate their history during the Choctaw Indian Fair, which is held once a year in June. The fair allows the Choctaw to exhibit their rich cultural past and celebrate with friends and family.

Mardi Gras festivities and parades are celebrated along the coast in January or February. Mardi Gras means "fat Tuesday" in French. It is traditionally celebrated the night before **Ash Wednesday** to greet the religious season of **Lent**.

QUICK FACTS

A traditional southern feast consists of such treats as pork tenderloin, fried chicken and okra, and pecan pie. Hush puppies, which are fried balls of cornmeal batter, are another southern treat.

Vietnamese settlers along the Gulf Coast hold many celebrations of their culture and provide other Mississippians with a taste of Vietnamese tradition.

The Choctaw are known for their brightly colored and beaded clothing.

ARTS AND ENTERTAINMENT

Many of the finest musicians in the United States are from Mississippi. Perhaps the most celebrated Mississippian is Elvis Presley. Elvis is famous for popularizing rock music, as well as for his acting career. Elvis Presley's music combined country and western music with rhythm and blues to create a truly distinct sound.

Jimmie Rodgers is another important musician. He is often regarded as the "Father of Country Music." Rodgers is known for his use of yodeling, steel guitars, and blues-influenced singing in country music. Jimmie was one of the first people inducted into the Country Music Hall of Fame.

Mississippi has erected a memorial to country music's first recording star, Jimmie Rodgers.

QUICK FACTS

John Lee Hooker is a famous blues musician. His first musical instrument was an inner tube played on a barn door.

In 1930, William Grant Still composed the *Afro-American Symphony*. It was the first major symphony written by an African American.

Leontyne Price, of Laurel, was the first African American to achieve stardom in the opera.

Actor James Earl Jones was born in Arkabutla, Mississippi in 1931. His booming voice is recognized around the world. He is the voice of Darth Vader in the *Star Wars* movies and, more recently, the voice of Mufasa in *The Lion King*.

Elvis Presley received his first guitar on his eleventh birthday. Two years later, he moved with his family from Mississippi to Memphis, Tennessee, igniting Elvis's music career.

The Blessing of the Fleet is an annual celebration that marks the start of the shrimp fishing season.

Some of Mississippi's most popular festivals celebrate the catfish and shrimp industries. The Shrimp Festival at Biloxi is held each June at the beginning of the shrimping season. It includes dances, parades, and the crowning of a Shrimp Queen. The World Catfish Festival in Belzoni also crowns a queen, Miss Catfish.

Museums and art galleries throughout Mississippi celebrate the state's culture and history. The major art gallery is the Mississippi Museum of Art in Jackson, but there are also many smaller galleries throughout the state. Tourists often make a special trip to Ocean Springs to see the art of Walter Anderson, the famous Gulf Coast painter.

Another notable Mississippi artist is Jim Henson who was born in Greenville. Henson created all the puppets for the television show *Sesame Street*, as well as the puppets for the famous *Muppet Show*.

QUICK FACTS

Oprah Winfrey was born in Kosciusko, Mississippi. She is now one of the most famous talk show hosts in the world.

Some of the best works of twentieth-century American literature have come out of Mississippi. William Faulkner was a Nobel Prize-winning author, and Tennessee Williams was a famous playwright.

Jim Henson came up with the word "Muppets" by combining the word "marionettes" with the word "puppets."

Tennessee Williams

SPORTS

Mississippi's many rivers and lakes provide plenty of opportunity for water skiing, swimming, sailing, and fishing. The Tennessee-Tombigbee Waterway is lined with beaches, campgrounds, and **marinas**. Miles of sandy beaches along the Gulf Coast are also great for water sports and other beach activities.

State and national parks provide hikers and cyclists with many exciting trails to explore. Some of the most exciting outdoor adventures can be found on the Gulf Islands National Seashore. The National Seashore preserves four islands off the eastern Mississippi coast.

Completely isolated, Horn Island is a preferred spot for the adventurous. In fact, the only way to get to Horn Island is by private boat. The island itself is a 3,650-acre strip of wilderness with forests, lagoons, and miles of deserted beaches.

Fishing is a popular pastime in Mississippi's many lakes and rivers.

QUICK FACTS

Biloxi's beach is the longest artificial beach in the world. It stretches for 26 miles.

Each September, Biloxi hosts a sand sculpture competition.

The Checker Hall of Fame is in Petal. Checker players from around the world go there for checker tournaments.

Many great athletes have come out of Mississippi. The Mississippi Sports Hall of Fame recognizes many of them. Its displays include tributes to football greats Brett Favre and Jerry Rice.

College football and basketball are also popular in Mississippi. Another popular team sport is stickball. It may be the first team sport ever invented. The Choctaw were among its first players. Stickball is still played on the Choctaw Reservation. Spectators can watch a stickball competition during the annual Choctaw Indian Fair.

Stickball is a game the Choctaw have played since prehistoric times.

Quarterback Brett Favre was named the National Football League's Most Valuable Player three years in a row. Favre was born in Kiln, Mississippi on October 10, 1969.

QUICK FACTS

The University of Mississippi's sports teams are known as the "Ole Miss Rebels."

James "Cool Papa" Bell was a great baseball player from Starkville, Mississippi. Although he never played in the major leagues, his lifetime batting average was an impressive .341. In one season alone, he stole 175 bases and is rumored to have once rounded all the bases in 12 seconds.

Sam Vick was a talented baseball player from Oakland, Mississippi. He played for the New York Yankees and the Boston Red Sox. He was the only man ever to **pinch-hit** for the famous Babe Ruth.

Brain Teasers

1

TRUE OR FALSE?

The teddy bear was named after President Theodore Roosevelt while he was on a trip in Mississippi.

Answer: True. While hunting in Sharkey County, President "Teddy" Roosevelt refused to shoot a bear. He earned the nickname "Teddy Bear," and soon the famous teddy bear was created.

2

What important artifact is on display at the Old Spanish Fort Museum in Pascagoula?

a. The world's largest pecan

b. The world's largest magnolia

c. The world's largest shrimp

d. The world's largest casino

Answer: a. The world's largest shrimp can be seen at the Old Spanish Fort Museum.

3

Which of the following are towns in Mississippi?

a. Alligator

b. Chunky

c. Hot Coffee

d. All of the above

Answer: d. All are towns in Mississippi.

4

TRUE OR FALSE?

Charles Walker, a checker player from Petal, Mississippi, once played 306 checker games at one time.

Answer: True. Walker won 300 games, tied five, and lost only one.

5 TRUE OR FALSE?

Jackson has always been the capital of Mississippi.

Answer: False. Jackson became the capital of Mississippi in 1822. Earlier capitals were Natchez, Washington, and Columbia.

6

Which soft drink was invented in Mississippi?

a. 7-Up®

b. Barq's Root Beer®

c. Pepsi®

d. Cream Soda

Answer: b. Edward Adolph Barq Sr. invented Barq's Root Beer in Biloxi in 1898.

7

The man who founded Hattiesburg named the town after:

a. His wife

b. His dog

c. His mother

d. His hat

Answer: a. Hattiesburg was founded in 1882. It was named after Hattie Hardy, the wife of a rich lumberman.

8 TRUE OR FALSE?

The world's first human lung transplant and the world's first heart transplant were both performed in Mississippi.

Answer: True. The University of Mississippi Medical Center conducted the first lung transplant in 1963. In January 1964, Dr. James Hardy conducted the first heart transplant.

FOR MORE INFORMATION

Books

Fradin, Dennis Brindell, and Judith Bloom Fradin. *Mississippi.* Sea to Shining Sea series. Chicago: Children's Press, 1999.

George, Charles. *Mississippi.* Chicago: Children's Press, 1999.

Ready, Anna. *Mississippi.* Hello USA series. Minneapolis: Lerner Publications, 1993.

Web sites

You can also go online and have a look at the following Web sites:

State of Mississippi
http://www.state.ms.us

Mississippi Web Pages
http://www.mde.k12ms.us/ms.htm

Choctaw Home Page
http://www.choctaw.org/

Official City Sites: Mississippi
http://officialcitysites.com/Mississippi.htm

Some Web sites stay current longer than others. To find other Mississippi Web sites, enter search terms such as "Mississippi," "Jackson," "Gulf Coast," or any other topic you want to research.

GLOSSARY

abolished: to do away with

alluvial: deposits of clay or sand left by flowing water in a valley or delta, usually producing excellent soil

Ash Wednesday: the first day of Lent

barge: a long, flat-bottomed boat, commonly used for carrying materials on canals or rivers

circumference: the outer boundary of a circle

civil rights movement: the struggle in the 1950s and 1960s to provide racial equality for African Americans in the United States

combines: harvesting machines that cut down crops

erosion: the wearing away of rock and soil

fertile: producing abundant vegetation or crops

floodplains: low-lying grounds that are near rivers and are subject to flooding

gullies: small valleys

Lent: the eight weeks before Easter; typically a period of fasting

levees: walls of stone or earth built to prevent the overflow of a river

marinas: docking areas for boats

pinch-hit: to substitute one player for another at bat in baseball

plantation: a large estate or farm on which crops such as cotton are grown

recruiter: a person responsible for bringing new members into an organization

segregation: forcing separation and restrictions based on race

silt: fine sand, clay, or other material carried by running water and deposited on land

topsoil: the fertile, upper part of the soil

INDEX